# SORRY

by Laura Alden
illustrated by
Dan Siculan

Distributed by
Standard Publishing,
Cincinnati, Ohio 45231.

ELGIN, ILLINOIS 60120

## Note to parents and teachers:

Using good manners helps to develop and maintain relationships. Saying words of apology or exhibiting an apologetic attitude shows respect and concern for the needs and feelings of others. That kind of caring should be the hallmark of Christian witness.

This book presents situations in which the word or spirit of "sorry" may be said or exhibited effectively. Use these situations to promote discussion. Help children identify with the situations and define their feelings, in order to apply the idea of "sorry" to their lives.

Distributed by Standard Publishing, 8121 Hamilton Avenue, Cincinnati, Ohio 45231.

**Library of Congress Cataloging in Publication Data**

Alden, Laura, 1955-
  Sorry.

  (What does it mean?)
  Summary: Presents situations, in pictures and rhyme, in which someone behaves in such a way that an apology is needed, and is usually accepted.
    1. Apologizing—Juvenile literature.
[1. Apologizing.  2. Forgiveness.  3. Conduct of life]  I. Siculan, Dan, ill.  II. Title.
III. Series.
BF575.A75A43  1982          158'.2          82-9660
ISBN 0-89565-236-6

1 2 3 4 5 6 7 8 9 10 11 12 R 89 88 87 86 85 84 83 82

# SORRY

''. . . and forgive us our sins,
just as we have forgiven those
who have sinned against us.''
—Matthew 6:12 [TLB]

I'm sorry.
Why, Lord, is that so hard to say?

First I said: it's not my fault.
Then I said: my sister made me.
I was angry all afternoon,
with my sister, with everybody,
with myself.

Then I said: I'm sorry.
Now I'm happy with everybody,
with myself,
and with you, Lord.
Amen.

—Madeleine L'Engle

# When you say,
# "I'M SORRY,"
## others know you care about them.

The leaves and I
fell in a heap
      on top of and over
      each other.

And before I thought
about how leaves fly,
      I threw some way up
      in the wind.

The leaves blew back,
all over a man
      who looked from between them
      and sighed.

"I'm sorry," I said,
brushing leaves from my head.
      Smiling,
      he went on his way.

Anne drew a picture
—carefully—
of her pet cat, Emily.
She gave it to me
to carry and keep.

I dropped it
—accidentally—
into a pothole puddle
of water and mud.
The picture was drowned.

"I'm sorry," I said.
Anne blinked away tears,
but she nodded.
She understood.

The calendar said,
"Dentist at 10."
Mom waited at the door.

"Do I have time
to brush my teeth?"
I hollered down the stairs.

"You did," Mom said.
"We're late. Come on!"

The car clock read,
"Two minutes to 10."

"I'm sorry that I'm late,"
I said.

# BEING SORRY

means making things right again.


The prayers, the hymns, the announcements
    were long. And we still had the sermon to go.
So we started to whisper to each other
    and laugh. Sometimes it's hard to be still.

After the service, Mom took me aside
    and told me I should apologize to
Mrs. Hammer. She couldn't hear because we
    were making so much noise.

So Jed and I apologized. And, better yet,
    next week we'll try to be quiet— and listen.

Leaping and kicking
sand in the air,
we ran down the beach
side by side.

Milton ran fast
  and out of control,
    though I tried to make him
    behave.

    Over the dunes,
      down to the shore,
        right toward some kids and
        a castle!

        SMASH! Milton crashed it.
        The kids were all mad.
          Their towering castle was
          totaled.

I called Milton back.
  I said we were sorry.
    And they let me help them
    rebuild.

"Cheater!" I yelled
when he won the game.
        Of course,
        I didn't mean it.

But Jared's eyes got big
and sad.
        He was hurt,
        and I felt bad.

Later, when we went to bed,
I whispered in the dark,
        "I love you,
        and I'm sorry."

"I love you, too," he said.

Sometimes,
# FEELING SORRY
helps you learn from your mistakes.

Shouts, shots, and pops
came from the show
that we were not to watch.

"All right," said Mom.
"Who turned on the TV?"

I had done it,
but I looked at Jared.

"Jared," Mom said.
"You know better than that—"

"I did it," I said,
and apologized,
as I should have done.

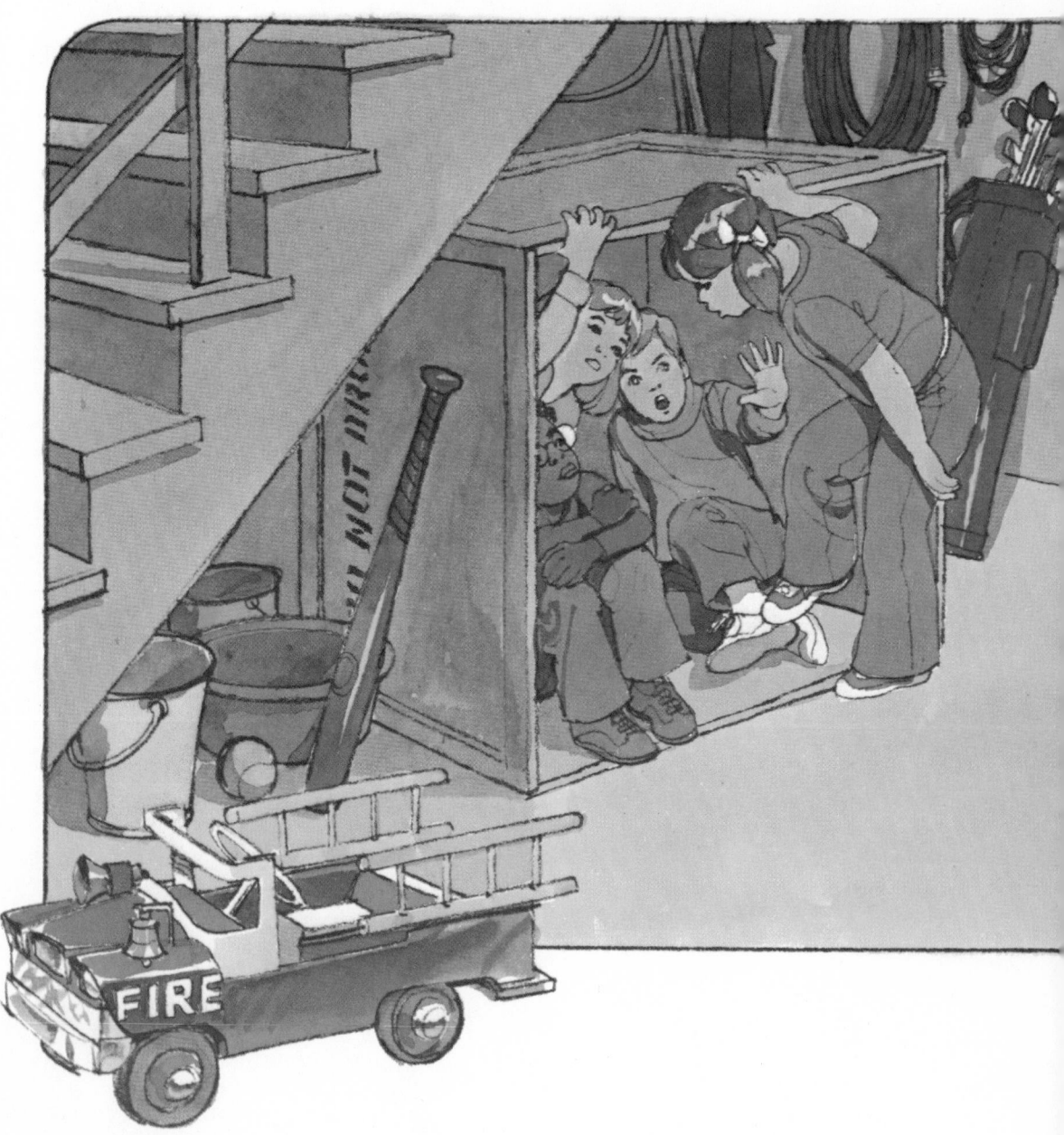

SARDINES!
We hid in a box in the basement.

Carrie found us . . . .
    Watch it! . . . OUCH!
She stepped on me (hard!)
    and I said,
"Carrie, you are too fat for this box!
    Get out!"

She started to cry
    and it was my fault.
I won't ever do that again.

Company was coming
in an hour.
"Don't mess up the house," Dad said.

I read for awhile
but then I got bored—
and, somehow, forgot what Dad said.

When the company came,
I had finished a fort
and really messed up the room.

I looked up at Dad.
I could tell he was mad.
"Sorry," I said. "I forgot . . . ."

"I'll talk to you later," Dad said.

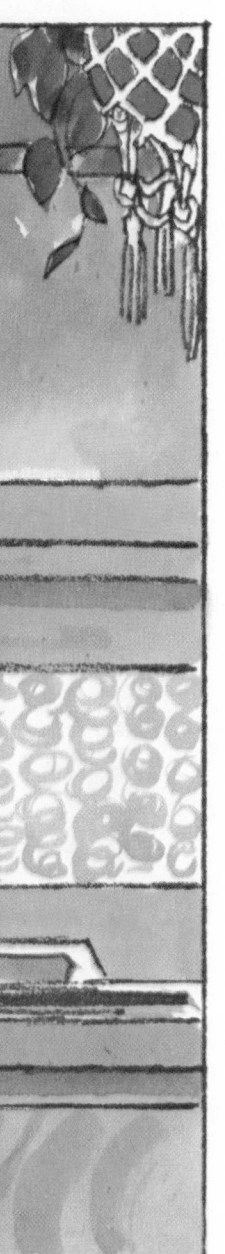

I couldn't wait
to talk to Mom,
though she was
on the phone.

I
INTERRUPTED
HER
AGAIN!

"Sorry," I said.
When <u>will</u> I learn?

# What do you do when
# OTHERS ARE SORRY?

I told them
　　not to play with my train.
I told them
　　to ask me first.

But they didn't ask,
　　and the switch came off.
The train is down, derailed.

I told them
　　not to play with it.
I told them
　　to just ask.

"Sorry," they said.
　　And I knew they meant it.
"It's okay," I said.

God,
There are lots of things
for which I should say I'm sorry.
And there are some things
I should forgive.

Help me do both.
Help me be kind.
And thanks for Your help
and Your love.

                              Amen.

**About the Author:**

Laura Alden holds a degree in communications and journalism from Bethel College (St. Paul, Minnesota). Her major professional interest and experience has been in children's publishing, in both the magazine and book fields. She is presently an editor for The Child's World, a publishing company that specializes in materials for early childhood. Ms. Alden lives in the Chicago area but thinks about Iowa a lot.

**About the Artist:**

Dan Siculan studied art fundamentals at the Oglebay Institute in Wheeling, West Virginia, and life drawing at the American Academy of Art in Chicago. His career began while in the army where he served as an artist while stationed in Europe. Mr. Siculan later worked as a commercial artist, becoming free lance in 1951. He is proficient in painting in oils, acrylics, and water color media and has produced numerous editions of original serigraphs. He is married and has four children and three grandchildren.

1317